Gloves Off

Essays by

Robert Laird

ISBN: 9781793819796
First Edition
©The Hurley Press, Camden, NJ
Elsinboro
Salem
Greenwich

Dedication

Glenna Leone Miesse (1922 – 2004)

My mother died the year after the last piece in this little collection was written. I haven't written much about her before because I was determined from the start to keep my family's privacy intact even in my fiction. Tired of reading about other writers' mothers and all the neuroses and obsessions they've instilled in their little boy scribes. But I've decided to talk about my mother here because in the particulars of her life she is an irrefutable proof of the fact that an important part of American culture is now gone, probably forever.

I've had problems in my life, like everyone else, but she didn't cause them. I did. Some were effected by the taking of necessary risks, others as the inevitable consequences of what I was and who I had to be. Both my parents did as much as they could to prepare me for storms ahead. They weren't always right, and neither was I. But my childhood was a good deal happier than most I've read about or heard tell of. My mother was a huge part of that happiness.

My dad had brains and breeding and an unbreakable moral backbone. My mother had brains too, but she poured her intelligence through an astoundingly diverse assortment of interests, skills, and emotional depths that made her a great and fine person. If I list the things she could do, it will sound like she was a domestic polymath, which I guess she was, but we never thought of her in resumé terms.

She could — take a breath and go, Robert —
knit Irish sweaters, sew skirts and dresses
and suits for my sister and herself (as well as
curtains and bookbags), upholster chairs in
leather and vinyl, repair worn out stitching in
leather seats, design and sew slipcovers for
chairs and sofas, cane chairs, do crewel
embroidery (drapery size), paint, varnish, and
shellack any wood you got, rewire lamps and
electrical outlets, unscrew broken lightbulbs
from lamp sockets, install hook-and-eye
latches, install wood hinges, make lamp
shades, hang wallpaper, and paint every room
in the house if there was no one there to help,
including the tricky moldings and trim work.
She could also sing (as in carry a tune to a
real song), dance the ballroom steps at the
country club, hit a mean forehand in tennis,
swim like a lifeguard (which she was in her
youth), explain why the batter who grounds to
short is almost invariably out at first base,
brush every inch of a cranky West Highland
White terrier, drive a four-speed manual
transmission (like her 1965 Mustang had),
and still get by in Paris with her college
French from 20 years ago — did I mention she
majored in Romance languages at Ohio State,
worked as a translator and also served in a
language capacity for what she only learned
after the fact was the Manhattan Project? Well
she did. French, Spanish, and Portuguese. So
much for the provincial Ohio girl label.

Now the thing about all these activities (skills, knacks, whatever word you prefer) is how they fitted into her life. She wasn't a Martha Stewart hunting down merit badges of cleverness. She learned how to do things as the need for them, or her perception of opportunity as need, arose. A lamp stopped working. The cord was old and frayed. New lamps were more than she wanted to spend (Scottish streak was strong), and it didn't look that hard to fix. Seat in a cane chair wore out. Hmm. Perfectly good chair. Can't be that hard... then pans of water with cane soaking, pegs, strong fingers getting stronger pulling cane tight, and then on to the next thing.

What's hard looking back is where she found the time. She put more than 25,000 miles on a car every year because she was the one who did for both sets of parents, hers and dad's, who lived about 15 miles away and needed errands run and General Looking After. She also played a very strong admin and general support role at the small Episcopal elementary school my sister and I attended. It had a shoestring budget and an 18th century classroom building. She did all the stuff no one else had the time or know-how to. Yet she was always home when my sister and I got off the bus, unless her errands made it easier for her to take us home herself.

She was always busy but didn't seem stressed or anxious. She just motored along through the days, weeks, and years. She didn't nag, because she'd seen her mother do that, and my dad worked just as hard on his job and the outside care required for two or three acres of land in the country. They didn't fight. When she was mad, she banged pots and pans in the kitchen. When he got mad, he put things that seemed out of place away rather severely. That took care of the whole temper problem.

We had a lot of family time together most weekends. We always ate dinner at table in the dining room, and good manners, correct use of utensils, eating everything put before you, and state capitals were important. My sister and I were allowed to have opinions and they were listened to. They wanted to know what we were learning in school. I mean they really wanted to know. And there were plenty of jokes too.

My dad had a ritual of listing at dinner the dishes he was expecting for breakfast (he always ate one fried egg), and one Saturday Mother let him have it: corned beef hash with fried eggs on top, blueberry pancakes, country fried potatoes, buttered toast, apple pie á la mode, and tomato juice with a twist of lemon. The look in his eye was worth all her effort and he manfully ate as much as he could manage. We all helped, except with the corned beef hash.

They had friends, but no girls or boys nights out. No bowling leagues or softball teams. They socialized with their friends at cocktail parties, to which kids were normally invited along. Friday nights it was always just us, in the book-lined den, and we listened to Sid Mark's "Friday with Frank" on the radio. We weren't the only ones. The show was syndicated across the nation. We were allowed to watch TV, and evenings we often did that together too. We kissed both parents good night at bedtime, which was always the same time except on weekends when it was a *little* later. We never called her Mom; she didn't want us to. Maybe because she'd heard it whined at other mothers too many times. It was Mommy until we hit an age when Mother was what we preferred. Me first, of course.

Mother read Shakespeare to us kids when we were still in the crib. She thought if it sounded good to her it would sound good to us too. When I got a real longbow, she taught me how to use it without hurting myself (high school archery team) and forgave me when I unexpectedly killed a rabbit. I cried and she said I knew better now.

I know better about a lot of things because of her. Because of my dad too, of course, but these days everyone, especially women, seem to belittle the kind of life my mother had, the kinds of things she excelled at and brightened people's lives with. That's wrong. But it's getting impossible to find the kind of women who would prove to them how wrong they are about an ancient social contract that has not only been junked without much thought but is also actively derided as demeaning and oppressive.

Why this book is dedicated to my mother. Everything in it, one way or another, arises from the torn up American contract we've never even learned to appreciate, let alone celebrate.

Gloves Off

Table of Contents

Wednesday, November 15, 2000

In Response to a Question Emailed by a Friend:

What is going on with this crazy presidential election?

All right. The election.

From An Amerian Glossary:

Law. An enormous pile of books containing very specific, very carefully chosen words describing what is legal and what is illegal, thus providing a platform for lawyers to argue that whatever the words mean, they're just not clear enough to justify a decision against their client(s) in this particular case. See also *Legislation.*

Lawful. Full of law, subject to interpretation by lawyers.

Lawyers. Brilliant men and women of high principle and integrity, who work devotedly for justice on behalf of the Amerian people and/or their clients by translating the law into a meaningless pile of empty bullshit. See also *TV lawyers.*

From The Boomer Bible, *Book of Hallites*:

Chapter 8

For example, the whole constitution of the Most Chosen Nation on Earth is based on one overridingly important principle,

2 Namely, the principle that nobody can be trusted,

3 Which used to make people take a pretty active interest in politics,

4 Because of all the things they didn't trust,

5 Government was the thing they didn't trust the most.

6 But then things changed,

7 Because they finally figured out that the thing they didn't trust the most was each other,

8 Which was when they decided that it was the government's job to watch over everyone,

9 And especially the ones they didn't trust the most,

10 Like the rich capitalists who might steal everybody else's money if they weren't held in check,

11 And the poor losers who might get violent and destroy everything if their basic needs weren't taken care of.

12 And that's when the government hired a whole bunch of people like you to do the watching,

13 Which has worked out great,

14 Because now that they don't want to think about anything at all,
15 They kind of have to trust you,
16 Unless they're willing to get involved themselves,
17 Which isn't likely to happen,
18 Anytime soon.

Chapter 9

In short, you couldn't be in a better position,
2 Whether you do your job or not,
3 Which means that they'll ultimately accept whatever you do,
4 Even if they complain a lot,
5 Because you work for the government,
6 And who else can you trust in this Most Chosen Nation on Earth?
7 That why there's nothing you can't get away with,
8 At all,
9 As long as you remember a few simple guidelines.

And from An Amerian Glossary:

Executive Branch. The branch of government run by the Presdent, responsible for pandering to the Amerian people, collecting their money, writing their checks, and running the country by executive order when the Congress is too busy empeaching the Presdent to pass any legislation.
Executive Order. The means by which the Presdent runs the country without having to bother with Congress, the budget, or other bureaucratic restraints; he simply orders the Treasury Department to write a check and tells the payee how he wants the money spent. Cool.

15

* * * *

Thanks to the unending scandals of the Clinton administration, a new family of political tactics has been created, based on the rediscovery that the letter of the law can always be interpreted into advantageous meaninglessness. Not coincidentally, this was the means by which Hitler heisted the German government from the Weimar Republic. His entire reign was nominally a legal suspension of the constitution for the purposes of dealing with a national emergency without having to deal with the legislative branch.

I'm not saying that the current election crisis is itself a coup d'etat. Rather, it is an oddly quick second application of the mechanism developed by Democrats to survive the impeachment process. The mechanism is nullification of law by heaping so much negative minutiae on top of the law – including its language, procedures, enforcers, and legitimacy – that its animating spirit is progressively belittled and ultimately smothered. With all of the pyrotechnics we've experienced in recent weeks, who is still able to see that the entire Democratic Party position amounts to no more than a pitiful argument by anecdote: "If a single person was unable to vote his preference, for any reason, that is reason enough for rewriting the election laws of Florida from the bench, ex post facto." Uh, no it ain't. But aim enough unscrupulous lawyers at a black-and-white situation, and it is speedily reduced to a sticky gray goo that blinds or paralyzes everyone. That's how the President survived his trial in the Senate, and it's how the Gore team intends to capture the White House. An amazing one-two punch.

Strangely enough, from the standpoint of a Gore presidency, it may seem one day soon that he had to come to power in exactly this way to achieve the effective coup d'etat that may be waiting in the wings. Yet in the normal course of affairs, such a circumstance would appear to be a remote possibility, not one that could ever be planned as part of a deliberate increase in presidential power. Thus, one is so struck by the oddness of its appropriateness to the overall situation that there is a tendency not to analyze, not to look beyond the circumstance itself for an emerging pattern in which it is, somehow, an obvious necessity.

I believe, however, that the pattern is there. The explanation for the oddness of its timing – coming so quickly after the battering given the rule of law in the impeachment debacle -- probably lies in the collective unconscious of the American people. An urgent moral drama is being enacted on the center of our national stage, and we have this one brief moment – consistent with the rules of Greek tragedy – in which we might but probably will not call a halt. We have asked for this, whether we know it or not, and we will surely reap the harvest of whatever decision we make or do not make.

What is the essence of the drama? A long-delayed confrontation between the origins of the American democratic experiment and its current incarnation, 68 years after the New Deal. These are direct opposites. The founders sought to protect citizens from the worst of all evils: government. The post-New Deal 'liberals' seek to protect citizens from everyone and everything by means of the government. The notion, shared by most people, that there can be some working compromise between such polar opposites is naive. Structural opposites can exist in a state of constantly changing compromises, moving back and forth between the absolute limits set by the structural design. But the opposition we are considering here is not structural. It is philosophical. In this realm, nominal compromises are frauds; they exist as optical illusions only, mirages reflected from the surface of convenient words whose roots grow in utterly different soil. One cannot be half-Stoic and half Epicurean, half-capitalist and half-Marxist, half-Christian and half-atheist. Whatever rhetoric is used to

18

disguise the conflict does not resolve the conflict. The ideas are, by definition, at war with one another. They will surface, and perhaps not as philosophical imperatives, but as warriors in a battle for control of the operative structure. Because of the extended timeframe over which such battles are fought, people can be lulled into interpreting the war as a working compromise. The fundamental agreement that must characterize compromise is not present, however; regardless of the positions taken by the superficial manipulators at the political center, the war goes on until there is a clear victor and a clear conquest. This is the climactic event we are approaching now.

The roots of the notion that government exists to protect people from everyone and everything are totalitarian, not democratic. It is worthwhile here to ask a question that has always been more interesting than its conventional explanation: Why were the founders so insistent about creating a clear line between church and state? The usual response – that they feared imposition of a state religion – is only a part, an example in fact, of the larger answer, which is that what they most feared was the power of a government that could claim to hold moral authority over the populace. In this direction lies ultimate tyranny.

19

I remember being taught the difference
between authoritarian governments and
totalitarian governments. (Interestingly, divine
right kingships were generally included in the
category of authoritarian governments, if for
no other reason than that totaliarianism was
regarded as a twentieth century invention
made possible only by advanced technology.)
Authoritarian governments exert control over
only those behaviors which affect their ability
to retain power; thus, they do not care what
people believe as long as they do not threaten
the legitimacy of the government. Totalitarian
governments exert control over everything,
expressly including what people believe,
because the most dangerous opposition
always arises from competitors to the moral
authority of the government; thus, Soviet
communism must outlaw the Catholic Church
and declare atheistic materialism as the
cosmological philosophy of the state. But why
must moral authority reside in the state itself?
Because such a system can retain its
legitimacy only by postulating all its actions to
be right automatically, in advance, because its
claim to be acting in the peoples' interest will
inevitably be exposed as a lie. The equality of
those outside the government is the equality of
slaves to a state whose every bureaucratic
twist and turn are law. And the greatest and
most obvious privilege of those who are part of

the government consists of relative freedom from the very bureaucracy that demands life-or-death obedience from the people at large. Such a state exists for its own sake only; therefore, it cannot tolerate any value system in which its hypocrisies might be visible.

Notably, the cornerstone of the constitutional edifice created by the founders in their attempt to preempt governmental tyranny was the rule of law. And it is expressly the rule of law which must be kept separate from the 'church,' however that is defined. For American jurisprudence was from its outset clear that the legal system was not a moral system per se; true justice was deemed the province of God in His infinite wisdom. The law was a parallel mechanism intended to exemplify morality rather than define it. And the law, in this context, would have to be absolutely governed by rules which might or might not result in justice, but which could be used to achieve outcomes that were approximately just, if the rules were followed and understood in their intent by carefully trained, morally upright practitioners of law. Why the separation? Two reasons. First, acceptance of the notion that true justice was not achievable by men meant that the more important (because more achievable) goal of the legal system was avoidance of gross injustice to innocents, even at the cost of letting malefactors go free. Second, postulating the law as an imperfect human mechanism made it clear that the state was ultimately less important and authoritative than the moral consensus of the populace. As a human invention, the law and its administration could become corrupt. In the same terms, the law could evolve and embody some forms of compromise that would not be possible if it were equated with the divine inspiration accorded to the Bible. It would not have to be right all the time; it would have to be consistent and fair in the application of its own rules. And, implicitly, it would be up to the people to decide when and if the law, and the government it framed, was failing in its moral duties to the populace by becoming corrupt, inconsistent, or unfair. Obviously, any government that could wrap its actions in an all-encompassing morality would no longer be accountable in this fashion. Thus, the rule of law – separate and unequal to the laws of God and the religious convictions of the populace. Still, there was one area of equality foreseen by the founders; that is, equality under the law for all citizens, regardless of rank, wealth, or other privilege. This was to be the prize that forgave the law its many inevitable errors and omissions. Acknowledged at the outset to be imperfect and far from divine, it would succeed in retaining the consensus support of a moral populace by continuously aspiring to justice, in accordance with rules that were the same for all. Not a bad bit of reasoning by a bunch of rich, Bible-beating ignoramuses...

Note that there is an essential humility to this approach. It is neither cynical nor prideful. It says, there is such a thing as justice, known in its entirety only by God, though it is our duty and our best hope to strive for it as best we can, overcoming our own imperfections by remaining aware of the difficulty of the undertaking and the abiding responsibility it entails.

What happens, however, if we remove God from this construct? Since justice resides ultimately in God, as example and arbiter of human affairs, without Him there can no longer be any justice; there is only the law. And without the continuous aspiration to justice on the part of the law's practitioners – which is to say, without the personal moral commitment to look past the letter of the law to the intent and spirit of the law – there remains nothing but words, words which can be stood on their heads by an agile mind that is bent on circumventing their obvious meaning.

It is here that the totalitarian roots of government as Supreme Protector come into play. The emotional basis of New Deal liberalism may have been compassion, but the worm in the apple is condescension. The intellect so disposed beholds the fact of rampant injustice in aspects of life never dreamt of by the founders as amenable to amelioration by the state. He beholds injustice in the very lot in life to which individual citizens are born – he beholds the millions who are ushered into life with unfair disadvantages of opportunity, intellect, talent, and cultural legacy. He does not ascribe this to God's will, because God has been removed from the construct by science. He ascribes it to chance, tradition, bigotry, and inaction by those who know better. He therefore defines a new moral ideal, one cast in strictly human terms, which comes to represent a mission whose ends justify the means employed by those who know better. From the peak of this new moral ideal, he condemns the mass of humankind for tolerating and abetting the perpetuation of such a priori inequality. And he therefore forgives himself in advance for what must to done to eliminate such inequality.

What has he done at this point, before he has even taken any action? He has moved himself into the vacant position once occupied by God. Now he is the example and arbiter; he is superior to human law; he is more than equal, in that he may commit, in the name of true justice, what other lesser humans may regard as sin; and he is not accountable to their definitions and beliefs because he has defined their legitimacy out of existence.

Most importantly, he has created a new construct in which the mass of humanity and the consensus that underlies their society are not an ideal to be served, but an obstacle to be overcome. He gives up easily on the challenge of converting them to his way of thinking, because such a conversion process would eventually lead to the declaration, "Trust me because I know better than you." He scorns accommodating his ideas to the legacy he has supposedly inherited, because he has already declared himself superior to that legacy. Thus, he is not in his private thoughts engaged in any exotic act of upholding the Constitution; he is bent instead on rewriting the Constitution to the extent necessary to make it conform to his self-anointed moral ideal. Yet he feels the weight of convention, the burden of the enduring stupidity of the masses. He knows that in order to prevail, he must appeal on a case-by-case basis to the self-interest of those he intends to help, confident that they will accept the figleaf cover of his rhetoric, and to all the others he is prepared to lie, misrepresent, and intimidate. Without the divine power of God, he must use his divine certainty with utter ruthlessness, always of course in the name of true justice.

He is committing an act of subversion. It is he who therefore inaugurates the war. His tactics are the tactics of warfare: divide and conquer. The goal is creation of a state which controls unto itself the definition of true justice and is equipped with the power to impose it. Since this is antithetical to the Constitution, the law which protects the right of the people to persist in their stupidity is a titanic, contemptible obstacle. In his head, he carries a running tally of old law versus new law; that is, the existing protections for what used to be revered as freedom, as opposed to the new powers and controls available to those who wish to put down bigotry, end inequality, and protect the helpless. He grows stronger as he passes more and more new law, which inevitably seeks to insert government into realms never contemplated by the founders: the workplace, the home, the family, the church (the latter reached by new laws of exclusion...). In the process, his contempt for all law increases. Old law is obstruction of true justice, the enemy to be smashed, circumvented, outwitted. New law is the pretext by which he moves closer to a vision of true justice that will grow ever more hungry for power.

Similarly, the "will of the people" is not a thing to be respected, revered, earned. It is a farce which can be and must be manipulated, used, created out of thin air whenever possible. His contempt for the actual "people" through time becomes so profound that he no longer counts it a lie to tell them what they must be told to accept the next step, the next law, the next initiative on their behalf. If they were not so hopelessly stupid, after all, they would not have to be dragged, step by step by step, to the relative paradise he is devising for them.

Throughout this evolution of political philosophy and practice, a metamorphosis has been underway. The moral idealist becomes by his own choices utterly corrupt. He will say and do anything to achieve the next increment of change. He will say and do anything to defeat his opposition, which is by definition immoral in its opposition to true justice. He reaches the point of no longer being able to recognize that anyone is operating by rules that are different from his own. Therefore, everyone else is also lying, misrepresenting, intimidating, dividing and conquering. The perfidy of their doing so in the name of evil justifies any and all means used to destroy them when they mount opposition of any kind.

Yet the veneer is maintained. The public words are of democracy, the Constitution, the will of the people, the American way. And the people do not recognize the war that is underway, ostensibly on their behalf. It is only when the stakes are truly large that the viciousness of the struggle leaks out into the open: the Bork hearings, the Thomas hearings, the impeachment, the 2000 presidential election. But even this is ultimately to the good, because in bits and pieces the people can be inured to the outrages that must be committed to the law, in the name of true justice. Gradually, they can be taught to understand that the law can and should be battered to pieces when it stands in the way of true justice, as defined by those with the loud, insistent voices. And when outright flouting and contempt for the law actually succeed in matters of national moment, they will learn a fairly easy part of the necessary lesson described below (from the Lounge Conversations, Loyerz Station):

As long as people continue to believe there is some moral component of the law, they will look to the law and the legal system to vindicate their own sense of what is right and wrong. Some will be tempted to pursue matters of principle through the courts. Others will be tempted to disobey laws they believe to be wrong. Still others will operate very close to the margin of the law, believing that they are in the right as long as they do not transgress the letter of the law. All of these behaviors reflect an intensity of individual spirit which is problematic in a country where all important decisions are made by bureaucratic committees and political compromises. You see, in exceptionally large and complex societal systems, the operating rules gradually evolve to a set that benefits the smooth functioning of the system. These rules do not correspond in any sense to notions of individual morality, which are not invented by committees but by human beings. The truth is that the most successful societal operating rules are pragmatic rather than moral. They retain an inefficient moral component only as long as there is sufficient individuality in the culture at large to pose a threat if the operating rules are perceived as amoral or anti-moral. It is therefore a necessary step for a self-aggrandizing system to eliminate the resolve of individuals to mount an opposition. The best way to do this is to make it clear that the law is not to be used, but to be feared. If being right ceases to matter in a court of law, the moralistic individual will learn to avoid the law like a contagious disease. He will learn to obey every law, no matter how foolish, follow every regulation, no matter how stupid, as if his life depended on it. Because it does.

Where do we stand in the ongoing war between the founders and the new moral arbiters? At the brink. The 2000 election divides the populace roughly in half, with a significant minority sitting somewhere in the middle between the two sides, without firm convictions about the major philosophical issue at stake. These are the ones who haven't thought about it, but it has already been proven that they can be controlled: this is the lesson taught by the majority opposition to removing the president from office for perjury and obstruction of justice.

The next president will therefore face a congress that is virtually doomed to partisan impotence. In his last year in office, Clinton has been dexterously pioneering a new form of executive governance; rule by executive order. This has gone virtually unnoticed. What better way to prepare the populace for a President Gore who will ultimately claim a mandate for ignoring Congress in favor of going directly to the "people" for support of rule by executive order, in the name of safety, compassion, and "true justice." It will cease to matter that he stole the election; he did it for the "will of the people," as polls will no doubt confirm. And should George Bush somehow persevere in nailing down the election he won, he will be so constantly accused of having stolen the election himself that the "will of the people' will be used by Democrats in Congress throughout his term to incapacitate government until the Democrats can be put in charge for good.

That's the plan anyway, as generously provided for by serendipity... or is it national destiny?

posted by Robert : 10:06 AM

Thursday, October 02, 2003

Al Franken is a Big Fat Splotchy... What?

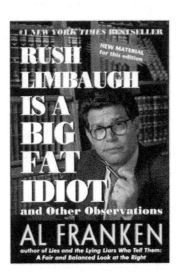

The claim seems to be that Al Franken writes satire. It's a claim worth examining because it leads to deeper questions about Franken and liberals in general. And the answers to those questions are more illuminating than anything Franken offers in his so-called satire, which is also revealing.

First, I should explain I have had a lifelong interest in satire as a literary form. I've read the great practitioners of this art – Swift, Voltaire, Twain, Bierce, Waugh, Orwell – not just as a consumer of their ideas but as a student of their skills and techniques. I concede up front that I disagree with Franken's politics; however, I have resisted giving in to my political reaction, which was to fight fire with fire by writing a satirical response of my own, because my intuition tells me there is more going on here than politics. Or perhaps there isn't. At any rate there is something at work in Franken's latest books which inclines me to reverse my field and fight fire with cold reason. Thus, this essay – an attempt to identify the elusive sources of my unease with Franken's methods and results.

The 'Limbaugh' and 'Lies' books don't strike me as satire. That's my beginning point. Why? That's the central mystery to be solved. They unquestionably employ some of the basic tools of satire, and much that conservatives find offensive in these works is nevertheless consistent with any good definition of satire.

For example, the satirist has no obligation to be fair. He has the right to select his content, arbitrarily if he so chooses, and plant it into a context of his own making for the express purpose of making the familiar unfamiliar and the (seemingly) reasonable absurd. He can be outrageous, shocking, and offensive. He can be as heated as he wants, and he can even employ ad hominem attacks if he deems them useful, though there are undeniable risks associated with both heat and and ad hominem tactics. He has no obligation to be funny; George Orwell's 1984 is brilliant satire, but it's not exactly filled with yucks.

The point has been made many times that it's counterproductive to analyze humor, because the very act of analysis slays its target; that is, humor thought about too much is no longer funny. As it happens, this phenomenon is one of the most effective tools for distinguishing satire from humor. Satire can be analyzed because unlike humor, it is primarily a function of reason. Confusion arises from the fact that humor is one of the most powerful weapons in the arsenal the satirist uses to achieve his objectives. But it's not the only weapon, and as we've seen, it's not a necessary one.

So far, none of the elements we've considered raise any particular obstacles to regarding

Franken as a satirist. It's immaterial that conservatives find him offensive, unfair, and unfunny. These responses might even be considered proof of his success. Yet this circumstance is precisely why it's imperative in Franken's case to employ a rational, analytical approach. Reason requires us to ask: Does the mere fact that a piece of writing is offensive, unfair, and unfunny constitute proof that it is satire? And the answer to this question is no.

Satire is permitted to be offensive, unfair, and unfunny as long as it achieves its single non-negotiable objective, which is to make the audience think and, hopefully, rethink its point of view about the subject topic(s). It doesn't have to achieve this objective with every member of the audience – only with those whose minds can be reached or reopened with ingenious uses of reason, which is the one weapon that must always be deployed in a work of satire.

Now the reason requirement is important because it leads us to the discovery that effective satire does have an obligation which is related to fairness, after all, though not synonymous with it. The obligation is to be consistent in the application of whatever rational model underlies and shapes the work. In other words, the prerequisite of satire is some rational description of what is right, correct, or appropriate. The satirist's weapons must be selected and employed for the express purpose of helping readers discover this usually unstated 'right description' by demonstrating the absurdity of any or all 'wrong descriptions.' Tactics that confuse the reader, obstruct his progress toward the 'right description,' or that give the reader good reason to doubt the soundness of this 'right description' are by definition failures of consistency that damage or destroy the satirical intent.

I apologize for the academic flavor of the discussion to this point; however, it has been necessary to show there is an academic component to satire. Humor may be a souffle. Satire, on the other hand, must be a kind of machine. It has working parts, a structure, an architecture, an overall design. Otherwise, it doesn't bear thinking about and fails. If it is, in this event, also offensive, unfair, and unfunny, that's all it is, no more worthy of consideration than a handful of mud slopped against a wall.

If Al Franken is a satirist, we must be able to discover a 'right description' that is illuminated by all the 'wrong descriptions' he targets with the weapons he has chosen to use. Moreover, this 'right description' must be inherently preferable to all the 'wrongs' and persuasively superior in absolute terms; that is, in terms that could be absolutely defended against the same kinds of weapons used to dismantle the 'wrongs.' Finally, the 'right description' defined by the satirist must possess a certain simple universality. Why? Precisely because it must be discoverable, appealing, and satisfying as an alternative to the various 'wrongs,' and it cannot be vulnerable to any of the attacks which define the 'wrongs.'

The process of writing thoughtful satire tends to be an uncomfortable one for the satirist. If he is honest, he is continually measuring and refining his 'right description' as he subjects it to the same kinds of attacks he levels against the 'wrongs.' This is how he arrives at universality. If he is fair in terms of his assessments, he winds up discovering errors and contradictions in his own assumptions; he experiences an unwelcome compulsion to attack various of his own traditional viewpoints and allies. He finds himself becoming more remote from specific thrusts and parries in the arena he is exploring, because the set of elements which can defended absolutely against all the attacks he can make is actually quite small. The definition of universality consists only of what he cannot destroy by the means available to him. The composition of the satire is thus a journey of self education and self criticism. If the satirist is not himself changed by that journey, he has probably accomplished nothing.

An excellent example of this journeying aspect of satire can be found in Voltaire's Candide. His beginning point is the optimistic philosophy of his age, as espoused by Leibnitz, whose ideas Voltaire recapitulates as "all is for the best in the best of all possible worlds." It would have been sufficient to poke a few gaping holes in this platitude. But Candide does far more than that, as if Voltaire was relentlessly scouring his own mind and experience for something, anything, that would arrive at a destination short of the platitude's exact opposite: all is for the worst in the worst of all possible worlds. And one might argue that the 'right description' he leads us to is just barely short of that destination: "il faut cultiver notre jardin" (we must cultivate our own gardens) is a very small island of potential meaning and fulfillment, but it's the only one he cannot destroy with his own potent weapons of reason.

There are, of course, some ways in which the satirist can simplify or minimize the journey and the self education associated with it. He can, for example, cast his 'right description' in very narrow terms. This is the stratagem generally employed by newspaper satirists like Russell Baker and Art Buchwald. However artful and sophisticated their weaponry, their product is the lowest form of satire; its 'right descriptions' tend to be mere opposites of their 'wrong descriptions.' They choose a position for or against some policy or person, construct an assault aimed at highlighting the weaknesses of the 'wrong' side, and the reader draws the obvious inferences about the unstated 'right.' There is a rational point to it, but the point is usually so slender that it sometimes seems no more than an excuse for the exercise of humor.

A variation of this approach that often results in considerably larger works consists of selecting a 'right description' that is from the outset so simple and self evident that it doesn't have enough specific gravity to warp the satirist's assumptions during the writing process. This stratagem tends to result in very pyrotechnical attacks against what in the end prove to be easy targets. The same villain is slain again and again and again – here garrotted, there exploded with dynamite, now shot in the face, then poisoned with cyanide, and so forth. The reader may be dazzled by the writer's display of weaponry, but his discovery of the 'right description' does not lead to thinking/rethinking so much as a disappointed 'So what?' An example of this kind of satire is Joseph Heller's Catch-22. The right description, "war is insane," is not much of a discovery. There's nothing wrong with enjoying the book for its spectacular creativity and humor; it's just that as a satire, its end point tends to be more self-congratulating than thought-provoking: "Yes, I agree that war is insane. How enlightened and sophisticated I am to be in accord with so brilliant a writer."

There's a particular pitfall associated with this kind of satire that is important to recognize. The danger of selecting a simple and self-evident 'right description' lies in the possibility of inadvertently settling upon a platitude so generic that it actually represents a half-truth, meaning that its sense of rightness is derived more from point of view than from any rigorous process of reason. When this is the case, for a certain percentage of readers, the 'right description' will collapse into a perhaps unintended and different, though more basic, 'right description.' Here again Heller makes for an interesting example. In hindsight, it looks very much as if Heller discovered this phenomenon of collapse in his own work and followed it stage by stage to progressively lower common denominators – war and the military are insane — all organizations, including corporations, are insane – all human efforts, including the best intentions of liberal governments are insane – life is insane. Of course, this final step takes us into the realm of nihilism, where reason avails nothing, and there is no help to be found and thus no point in the satire. It becomes black comedy, a mere existential exercise, at which point any uses it makes of moral outrage or discriminating definitions of justice are reduced to irrelevant, showy accessories – a diamond stickpin on a concrete overcoat.

The defense against this kind of vicious circle is easily seen in truly effective satire. When we arrive at Voltaire's "il faut cultiver notre jardin," we have reached a new beginning point. What does this mean in terms of my own life? What is my garden? How should I be cultivating it? The learning process of the book leads us to a new learning process in terms of individual decision making. This is the elusive objective for which satirists strive in the journeys they map out in words.

What is the journey we undertake with Al Franken? What is his 'right description'? If we begin with his most recent work, which presumably represents the pinnacle of his own philosophical development to this point in his life, we are permitted to draw inferences from the title: Lies and the Lying Liars Who Tell Them. At least as a working assumption we can infer that his 'right description' relates to truth. That seems promising. It sounds rather grand. Truth. What about it?

For the moment all we have to do is accept that his 'right description' pertains to truth. All the 'wrongs' he will eviscerate with his satirical weapons will fill in the details of his 'right description' by showing us what cannot be included in that description by virtue of belonging to the 'wrong description.' His choice of weapons will also provide us with information about his 'right description' because we will discover something about the importance of his 'ends' by observing what 'means' are acceptable in pursuing them, and indeed, if there be any such thing as a means which is not acceptable.

The first thing that cannot be allowed in the 'right description' is, apparently, errors or misrepresentations of fact. It speedily becomes clear that the author has mustered fairly abundant resources to document a long list of such errors and misrepresentations. He takes pains to identify such departures from truth, however he (and we) will ultimately define it, with specific individuals, including Bill O'Reilly, Ann Coulter, Sean Hannity, a variety of Republican politicians, and, of course, George Bush. He is, therefore, operating in the realm of nonfiction, which is permissible in satire. The choice of a nonfiction approach does, however, entail some additional risks and requirements which should be noted before we proceed further.

A satirist's choice of fictional devices of any kind is almost always a means of simplifying and clarifying the scope of the underlying idea or set of ideas. If the premise is wholly fictional as in, say Orwell's Animal Farm, it does not follow that the satirist is any less interested in directing our attention to specific events, situations, and people. It is child's play to pick out the historical figures of Lenin and Trotsky in Animal Farm, and Orwell very much desires us to do so. What benefits is he therefore seeking in his use of a fictional device, and what problems is he avoiding?

The primary benefit he gains is to eliminate most of the messy and complicating noise of the real-world history he is using as a vehicle to reach his 'right description.' He wants to separate his readers from the probably fragmentary and distorting context of what they may think they already know about that history. For his purposes it doesn't matter whether or not the Russian Revolution involved atrocities in its process of coming to power. It doesn't matter if Lenin was ugly or bald or had bad breath. He wants us to focus on the contest of ideas and character that were acted out in the establishment of the Soviet Communist model. He is simultaneously clarifying the focus of his attention and predisposing our perspective on the events and people he is recreating for us. Lenin and Trotsky are, for example, to be viewed as pigs.

The principal problem he avoids is creating unnecessary vulnerabilities in his renderings of events, situations, and people. There is nothing to be gained, and much to be lost, by depicting historical scenes about which there may exist factual disputes, multiple subtle interpretations relating to personalities, and external factors that probably did affect outcomes without illuminating the ideas with which Orwell is most concerned. He knows that every instance in which a reader can take issue with his factual reporting is a distraction, a detour from the most effective route to the destination he has in mind.

With this example before us, we can draw some pretty straightforward conclusions about Franken's decision to use an almost purely nonfiction approach to his subject. He is informing us by this choice that all of the messy noise of the real world is relevant to the journey he has charted for us. We are therefore permitted, perhaps even encouraged, to draw upon our own memories of the events, situations, and people he references, and he is so confident of the irreducible rightness of his 'right description' that he knows it will survive any distractions created by his reporting of the facts. Note that this represents a pretty enormous promise on his part, that he will be scrupulously accurate about the points which matter most. This is a promise which is amplified by an order of magnitude because the primary subject of his 'right description' has to do with truth.

The scale of the additional risk he is running with this approach can be understood if we recognize that he has, to all intents and purposes, accepted a requirement almost never needed in satire: the requirement to be fair. It is possible, of course, that his definition of fairness will differ from ours, but our journey will also educate us about that definition, which will be helpful in understanding his 'right description' about truth.

As we read the text, we discover almost at once that we were right in the main conclusions we've just drawn. In Franken's context, the circumstance that Lenin might be ugly and bald and have bad breath is relevant. In his prior work, we cannot escape the reality that to Franken, it is significant that Rush Limbaugh is fat. He repeats this fact many times. In the newest work it is important that Bill O'Reilly is 'splotchy.'

This is significant information for us, the readers. It enables us to assume that the 'right description' of truth has to do both with factual accuracy and physical appearance, or if we don't want to leap all the way to that conclusion, we can read physical appearance as a stand-in for the specifics of who and what people are, as opposed to their positions and statements about ideas. We can infer that truth has intimately to do with being.

We also know that Franken's decision to be specific about personal, physical imperfections is fair. This derives from the implied contract he makes with us in his choice of a nonfiction, real-world approach.

All right. He is operating in the real world, allowing in all of our preexisting knowledge such as it is about the topics he references. He is being fair, whether it appears that way to us at first blush or not. He is leading us to a 'right description' of truth that will not be violated or compromised by the weapons he deploys against the 'wrongs.' Where does our journey go from here?

Well, actually, it goes all over the place. It touches upon most public policy issues, including matters of budget, race, war, and almost anything else that can become a topic of discussion in the nation's political life. It takes in dozens of individual Republican or conservative targets, from media personalities to the president of the United States. It involves lengthy citations of what the author characterizes as lies, misstatements, and misrepresentations. It even ventures into areas where most readers would concede that a finding of fact rests far more upon untidy interpretations of complex variables than on clearcut yes/no data. For example, the decision to declare as fact that victory in Afghanistan is solely attributable to the military stewardship of the Clinton administration is presented as a triumph of Franken's logic, even though it clearly can be, and has been, disputed with seemingly strong counter-arguments by Republicans.

Perhaps this is an important clue about the 'right description' of truth in Franken's view. After all, he also informs us as baldly as if it were fact that there is no liberal bias in the mass media. In making such an assertion in the context of the real world, he is expressly acknowledging that other viewpoints exist, as they do. Most public opinion polls reveal that by very dramatic margins Americans believe that a liberal bias does exist in the mass media. Yet we know that this circumstance is also relevant to what Franken is telling us. Part of the lesson, therefore, must be, inescapably, that where our views of what the facts are differ from his, his are right, and ours are wrong.

The real world enters the picture in an even more significant way if we examine his lists of lies, misstatements, and misrepresentations in the context of messy history, the author's methods, and the overall tone of his presentation. The title of the book makes it clear that he is not just offended but enraged about the lies he has engaged so many resources to document. And yet his choice of nonfiction has allowed us, even required us, to recall our own experience of what we may consider unassailably proven facts about lies, misstatements, and misrepresentations during the two terms of the Clinton administration. He knows we may very well harbor such convictions, and even though we've been admonished to accept his statements of fact over our own, he absolutely must be aware that a reasonable person could conclude from his presentation that both sides of the great right-left, Republican-Democrat conflict tell lies. In fact, this could easily be the sign of an empty half-truth lurking inside the 'right description' he is leading us to.

Yet if that were the case, all the heat – the rage, contempt, and ridicule – he heaps upon his targets would be irrelevant. And no one could be so stupid as to write a whole book, backed by the blessings of Harvard University and more than a dozen of its best and brightest graduate students, in such a continuous state of venomous high dudgeon if there were any possibility whatsoever that its end result might be the "So what" conclusion that all politicians and their media advocates tend to tell lies that advance their interests of the moment.

No. This is a flat impossibility. Franken knows that we know that there is evidence of lying by Democrats and the Clinton administration. And since he specifically limns for us sprawling abstractions, such as the military

50

credit for victory in Afghanistan, which he is nevertheless confident about labeling as lies, it has to be the case that he is telling us something very new and different about the 'right description' of truth.

We have all the pieces spread out before us. Lies are disgusting, revolting, repellent things. Republicans tell long lists of lies, ranging from errors of fact to misinterpretations of complex issues. Their immorality in such matters makes it fair to pile abuse upon their motives, their characters, and even their physical shortcomings and defects. It is even fair to condemn them for piling abuse of a similar kind upon Democrats and to deliver such condemnations with all the self righteousness one would expect from a writer who has never engaged in such low practices.

Is there some key we can use to unlock the 'right description' at the heart of the book? Perhaps there is. At one point Franken pillories Ann Coulter for using end notes rather than footnotes in specifying the charges she makes against Democrats. Is it a coincidence that Franken employs the very same device to document his own charges?

It is not a coincidence. Indeed, all the available evidence points in the same direction. In this book Al Franken is cleaving the world in two, and different standards are to be applied to the two halves. Here is the only 'right description' which is consistent with all the content and all the 'wrongs' he attacks. The truth is what Democrats and liberals are. Lies are what Republicans and conservatives are. It is therefore appropriate to demonstrate what Republicans and conservatives are by enumerating instances in which they lie or can be accused of lying. Significantly, it is not appropriate to use documented lies to demonstrate what Democrats and liberals are, because such an exercise is entirely irrelevant to their unassailable definition as truth.

What more can we discover about truth in terms of this definition? Surely, the tone of hatefulness and bile is intended to lead us to a realization that this truth of Democrats and liberals is an absolute truth, which represents a 100 percent opposite of the lies which the Republicans and conservatives are. And Franken can be so completely confident and absolute in his own pronouncements for the simple reason that he also is a Democrat and a liberal. Everything he does is fair because the truth is always fair, and he is the truth (regardless of what the definition of 'is' is...).

Now that we have arrived at this core definition of truth, we can recollect that it is allowable and appropriate for us to flesh it out with our own knowledge, however imperfect, of the other attributes – e.g., beliefs, positions, behaviors, specific actions – of Democrats and liberals, because all such attributes represent some part of what they are and therefore what 100 percent truth encompasses.

Thus, if we examine what they are for, either from their own collective record or from a reading of what Republicans and conservatives are against, we will find the truth that we must all accept, whether or not we're inclined to hold dissenting views of any sort. We will know that we're on the right track if we find evidence in Franken's curriculum vitae that confirms the conclusions we draw.

For example, we can start with an easy one: abortion. Republicans are against abortion. They are convinced that it is murder or something very like it. But Republicans are 100 percent wrong. Therefore the truth is that abortion is not murder or anything like it, and there is no possibility of there being any question about this fact.

Republicans believe in God. In fact, they believe in a very specific God who has very definite views about what is right and what is wrong. But Republicans are absolutely wrong. Therefore the truth is that even if some

Democrats choose to believe in a God, it is a fact that God does not have definite views about what is right and what is wrong, unless it's the case that God's views are indistinguishable from the truth of the Democrats and the liberals. In either case, the Republicans are absolutely wrong in believing that some presence of God should be permitted in institutions of government, including the schools, because it is a fact that God must be eliminated from such institutions, as Democrat positions demonstrate beyond doubt.

Republicans believe that the increasing absence of God and his definite views on morality have precipitated broad cultural decay, marked by dangerous levels of sexual promiscuity, a pervasive coarsening of popular culture, a steep and accelerating decline of educational institutions and the professions, including law, medicine, and the academy. But Republicans are absolutely wrong. Therefore the truth is that even if there is some increase in sexual promiscuity it represents progress, and there is nothing wrong with having a coarse popular culture, and it's perfectly appropriate for the professions to attack and cannibalize the very institutions they were once sworn to protect. By the same token, it is perfectly fine and appropriate for Democrats to make the kinds of statements and representations that would be lies if they were uttered by Republicans or conservatives, because everything done or said by Democrats and liberals is fair, by definition, because it is right, since they are truth.

We could go on and on like this, fleshing out all the particulars of the incontrovertible truth, but it is perhaps more productive for us to check our reasoning against what we can know about Al Franken. We know we're right about the God part of the equation. He is on record as saying that he has "no formal religion." We know we're right about the truth of popular culture, because he has spent years helping to coarsen that culture by pushing the outside of the envelope on Saturday Night Live. And we know we're right about the absolute nature of his cleaving of the world in twain because he has told us that he would like the title of his next great work of satire to be "I F*cking Hate the Motherf*ckers." If you love humanity as profoundly as the Democrats and liberals do, which postulated love of humanity is of course part of the definition of truth, then it's a mighty strong message that half of the humanity in an entire nation can be deserving of such hatred. It means they must be 100 percent wrong about everything. Even if that doesn't seem possible. I mean, who are we to say about that? A key part of

The Truth is that only Al Franken has a right to say anything about it.

At this point we have accomplished one of two things. We have established that Franken's latest book is a complex, ambitious, and novel satire leading us to what is indeed a brand new beginning point for an individual learning process – or we have demonstrated that he is so incredibly stupid and shallow that he wasted the time of 14 Harvard graduate students and himself on a satirical point that is at best a half-witted half-truth whose rebuttal is assured in every scrap and line of invective penned by its impossibly arrogant and ignorant author.

Which do you think it is?

Friday, September 19, 2003

Enough is Enough.

*Greeley's no longer with us, so
I won't describe him as vulpine.*

It's time to recognize what Democrats call
political debate for what it is: vicious,
unprincipled demagoguery that provides aid
and comfort to the enemies of the United

States. I am by no means a kneejerk defender of the policies of the Bush administration. I believe there are many issues about which reasonable people can disagree, and I believe the country would benefit from a civil airing of competing ideas about how best to deal with the challenges we face. That is not what is occurring now.

If there was a straw that broke the camel's back, it was Andrew Greeley's column in today's issue of the Chicago Sun-Times. You can read the lede here (and the rest of the text at{http://www.agreeley.com/articles.html.) Greeley was so proud of this piece he put it on his 'best of' web page, at the top of the list of his most prized religious essays. Go figure.

One suspected interpolation I will point out. There's a breakout quote shortly after the lede highlighting Greeley's claim that he didn't necessarily believe Bush knew he was lying. I believe this an after-the-fact CYA, a revision of history undertaken long afterwards. Newspaper columns don't usually waste valuable column inches on breakouts.

Big lie on Iraq comes full circle

Published September 19th, 2003
in the Chicago SunTimes' Daily Southtown
By Andrew Greeley

Joseph Goebbels, Hitler's propaganda chief (director of communications, in the current parlance), once said that if you are going to lie, you should tell a big lie. That may be good advice, but the question remains: What happens when people begin to doubt the big lie? Herr Goebbels never lived to find out. Some members of the Bush administration may be in the process of discovering that, given time, the big lie turns on itself.

The president has insisted that Iraq is the central front in the war on terrorism, a continuation of the administration's effort to link Iraq to the attack on the World Trade Center. While almost three-quarters of the public believe that Saddam Hussein was personally involved in the attack, the polls after the president's recent speech show that less than half believe that Iraq is the "central front" of the war on terrorism. Moreover, the majority believe that the war has increased the risk of terrorism. A shift is occurring in the middle, which is neither clearly pro-Bush nor clearly anti-Bush. The big lie is coming apart.

There is not and never has been any evidence that Iraq was involved in the 9/11 attack. None. The implication of such involvement was an attempt to deceive, a successful attempt at the big lie.

He's a Catholic priest. He's also a disgrace.

He begins his polemic with a reference to Joseph Goebbels, the Nazi minister of propaganda who propounded the concept of the "Big Lie," the one which will be believed if it is repeated often enough. As a priest, he's far too diplomatic to put the words "Bush" and "Hitler" in the same sentence, but we'd have to be idiots to miss his intent. It's not as if this odious comparison originated with him. It's been repeated so often that it's become a motif of the left – the very same left which claims to own a monopoly on tolerance and which continually accuses itself of being "too nice" in its dealings with the Republican opposition.

Jonah Goldberg has written a brief and rather restrained analysis of the Bush-Hitler theme, which you can read at NRO. His essay makes the obvious (though evidently still necessary) point that such rhetoric is not only insulting to the nation and the president but also serves to trivialize the monstrous horror of the holocaust. He seems to think that identifying this fact might deter so-called liberals from persisting in their dishonest comparisons. Unfortunately, Mr. Goldberg is giving his opponents more credit than they deserve.

The truth is, Greeley and his kind cannot let go of the Hitler motif. There are several reasons why, and they are all revealing. In fact, they are so revealing that it's worth digging into them in considerably more detail than Jonah Goldberg probably felt necessary.

The History of an Evolving Falsehood

One of the most longstanding fallacies in American political culture is the identification of Nazism as a right wing phenomenon. The term "Nazi" is essentially an acronym for National Socialism, which was a political movement that positioned itself in opposition to what it regarded as weak representative democracy. Hitler's notion of the ideal state was as far away as it could be from the principles of limited government, personal liberty, and individual rights which typify Republican/conservative views in this country. He believed in big government, secular government (else why oppress and silence the churches), intrusive, controlling government embodying all the moral ideals of the nation. Does this not evoke more comparisons with American left/liberal ideology than with American right/conservative ideology?

Historically, it has been a clever trick of American Democrats to sneak Nazism's position on the so-called right wing of the Weimar Republic into a left-right spectrum of American politics defined by entirely different factors. Hitler was right wing in a German context because he was opposed to the brand new 'liberal' experiment with democracy in a country which had been ruled by a monarchy throughout its history. He was reactionary in wanting a government that returned to the strong controls of the past. At the exact moment that he was engineering his rise to power, however, the reactionary thrust in America was in the opposite direction: to return to the weaker, less intrusive central government which had obtained in America prior to the 1932 quasi-revolutionary turn toward big government known as Franklin Roosevelt's New Deal.

Lots of additional Democrat sleight of hand parlayed this initial misrepresentation into an accepted cliche. Hitler's opposition to Communism helped American liberals to reinforce his position as a rightwinger. But this was also a spurious inference. Hitler opposed the communists not because his totalitarian approach to government differed in any material way from that of Lenin and Stalin, but because communism was internationalist by definition, which was incompatible with the mission of German empire. Still, with this double layer of falsehoods in place, it became easy for Democrats — long after the war — to depict Republican antipathy to communists as fascism, i.e., Nazism, and subsequently to equate Republican resistance to sweeping federal Civil Rights legislation with Nazi racism and genocide.

All such associations were primarily rhetorical devices; Nazism/fascism was a convenient bucket of tar that could be used to smear any Republican or conservative who opposed Democrat positions on social and foreign policy matters. The continuing fringe existence of the Ku Klux Klan enabled canny Democratic politicians to characterize all Republican positions as veiled manifestations of Hitlerian supernationalism and racism. Lost to us now in these days of historical ignorance and amnesia are the original contexts for a variety of post-WWII Republican positions.

The symbolic rite of passage for 20th century American liberals was the period they have succeeded in labeling the "McCarthy Era." If Republicans had been half as rhetorically astute, we would in all likelihood know this time by a different name, as "The Era of Soviet Infiltration." The end of the Cold War has almost universally vindicated the charges by Republicans in the late 1940s and 1950s that Soviet espionage agents occupied critically compromising positions in multiple agencies of the U.S. government and the military. Despite the villainization of Richard Nixon, his target Alger Hiss was, we now know, guilty. The Rosenbergs were guilty. FDR's Chief of Staff Harry Hopkins was guilty. Staggeringly important secrets were passed by American citizens to the Soviets, including plans for both the atom and hydrogen bombs. There is simply no way to deny the truth that the communist conspiracy claimed by the Republicans did, in fact, exist and was consistently denied, dismissed, or provided cover for by the Democratic party.

Nevertheless, the liberal/left elite in this country has succeeded in perpetuating a dramatic myth that is flatly contradicted by the facts. The anti-communist crusade of Joseph McCarthy, by reason of its impoliteness and its incompetence, has become the secular Passion of liberalism, its sanctifying crucifixion, the basis of its arrogant, continuing, and utterly unjustified claims of moral superiority over the conservative opposition. (Lest you regard this as overstatement, please read "The Crucible," Arthur Miller's play about the McCarthyism of the 17th century Salem witchcraft trials — as we all know, there were no witches/communists . . .) We are supposed to overlook the enormity of the fact that at the very dawn of the nuclear age, American citizens conspired to transfer the deadliest technology ever developed to the mortal enemies of their country. This terrifying event is supposed to pale beside the prospect of a Hollywood screenwriter whose career was damaged by his membership in the 'party' that led the conspiracy. It doesn't — except in the minds of those who have never quite understood, and probably never will — the sickening, murderous evil that was the Soviet communist state.

Yet the Democrats won the word war. The term 'McCarthyism' entered the language and has been kept vigorously and determinedly alive. It is, by usage, synonymous with fascism, because it has come to mean the ruthless persecution and demonization of an imaginary enemy for purely political purposes. And ever since the great Democrat Passion of the 1950s, this word has been hurled at every concerted Republican attempt to uncover any kind of wrongdoing in the left/liberal establishment.

Another shoe dropped during the Civil Rights movement. Almost no one now remembers that many Republicans opposed the 1964 Civil Rights Act for reasons that had nothing whatever to do with racism. Partly this is occasioned by the fact that almost no one remembers where the core of virulently racist opposition to the Civil Rights Act reposed — in the Dixiecrat (i.e., southern) wing of the Democratic Party. Republicans who entirely agreed with the ultimate aims of the Civil Rights movement as they were then described — the G.O.P. was proudly the party of Lincoln, after all — nonetheless opposed the scope of proposed federal legislation that would dramatically reduce the rights of individual states to write their own laws. Thirty years of virtually uninterrupted transfers of power to the federal government gave Republicans pause; they opposed subsequent Medicare legislation for much the same reason: fear of a central government growing too big, too powerful, too intrusive, too expensive. Of course, to the most enlightened social progressives of the time it was impossible to allow that anyone might hold such a contradictory view; all opponents of the legislation had to be regarded as racists and were branded as such.

Once again, the tarring worked. How many American citizens know today that a higher percentage of Republicans voted for the 1964 Civil Rights Act than did Democrats? From this point forward, the Republicans were racists by definition (and by repetition) and were forever to be associated with a KKK whose most prominent members had been Democratic politicians.

A further subtle transition was accomplished during the antiwar movement of the late 1960s. The baby boomer leftists who opposed the Vietnam War traded the term 'McCarthyism' for the more general purpose 'fascism.' This was the period when it was impossible to walk across an elite university campus in America without being handed a smudged mimeograph denouncing the "fascist imperialist U.S. pigs . . ." Vietnam had started as Lyndon Johnson's war, but it fell to Republican Richard Nixon to find the way to end it. The fascist label was accordingly transferred to him in the blink of an eye, and it was precisely during this phase of the war that the antiwar movement migrated from opposition to treason, meaning open alliance with the North Vietnamese enemy, hysterical accusations of war crimes against U.S. soldiers, and even some cheering of the death and suffering of American troops. This was also the timeframe within which the left/liberal wing of the American political spectrum began to employ the term 'genocide' and proclaim it an instrument of American foreign policy. Not coincidentally, the same people transformed 'patriotism' into a term of opprobrium.

If the McCarthy Era was the left/liberals' crucifixion, Watergate was the resurrection. How serendipitously easy it was to caricature Nixon aides Haldeman and Ehrlichman as storm troopers . . . how remarkably convenient it was to conceal the repudiation of the left represented by the crushing defeat of George McGovern in the 1972 election underneath the mushrooming scandal . . . and how lucky it was that the consequences of the left's 'principled' stand against the war — i.e., the massacre of 2 million or more Cambodians — disappeared into the opera of Nixon's downfall. Yes, despite the Cambodian holocaust, American left/liberals now regarded themselves as wholly vindicated, and to this day they cling to the memory of Richard Nixon as if he were their own Shroud of Turin, the incontestable (if fraudulent) artifact of their self-anointing to political divinity. Nixon became the American Hitler they implicitly opposed in all Republican opponents, the one most evident incarnation of the demon they would always see and attack in every strong Republican leader — corrupt, conspiratorial, racist, and perversely opposed to every ideal treasured by the morally initiated, including the rights of women, children, minorities of every stripe, and specifically including all foreign enemies.

The Contemporary and Obsessive Uses of Falsehood

This entire history collapses into a single article of faith which can be transmitted to young recruits without much explication of the formative events. The article of faith is that the Republicans, especially conservative Republicans, are fascists at heart, ever slyly in search of ways to rob less privileged people of rights, opportunities, freedoms, and money. Thus, the image of Hitler springs easily to mind for people of so-called liberal persuasion. It is a deeply satisfying image, one they have used to considerable advantage, and (the dirty secret) they have learned much from their long association with it.

What have they learned? Precisely what Andrew Greeley references in the first sentence of his column: the efficacy of the Big Lie. This is a recurring theme in Democrat rhetoric precisely because they have used it so routinely and effectively for their own purposes. A more familiar term for it is the "spin" perfected by the Clinton administration, which consists of "talking points" to be used verbatim by every conceivable spokesman for the party. The mechanism is not truth, but repetition. If Republicans oppose automatic budget increases, they are "seeking drastic cuts in services" for needy men, women, and children. An increase in the school lunch program that is not as large as desired can be compared to "genocide." Concern that affirmative action programs may promote more resentment than genuine opportunity can be branded as "racism." All that's necessary is to repeat the charge ad nauseam, see that it spills out of every mouth that has access to a microphone, and eventually a significant percentage of the population will believe it.

More recently, Democrats have employed the Big Lie to carry Clinton through the disgrace of impeachment. For months, every available mouth repeated the mantra that "lying about sex isn't a crime because everyone does it," "lying under oath isn't necessarily perjury," and "breaking the law isn't necessarily an impeachable offense."

After the 2000 election, the Big Lie that has been repeated often enough to be believed by too many idiots is that "George Bush stole the election." Never mind that Al Gore broke an incredibly important precedent which even Richard Nixon was too principled, too patriotic, to defy. Even when confronted with strong evidence of vote fraud in Cook County during the 1960 presidential election, Nixon decided not to contest Kennedy in the courts for the good of the country. It was the feckless ambition of Al Gore which resulted in the electoral ordeal which will now, undoubtedly, be repeated in every close election from here on out. Yet who has stepped forward to imagine for us the implications of protracted legal battles in every state decided by fewer than several thousand votes, in perpetuity? The very first decision to contest the outcome in a single state inevitably awakened the possibility that all future national elections will end precisely where they never should, in the hands of politically appointed judges. We have Al Gore to thank for that. But where is the Republican attempt to use the "Big Lie" to drive home this dire fact with the American electorate? It doesn't exist. This particular tool has been transformed into a nuclear weapon only by the Democratic party and its leftist minions.

The appalling ugliness of the current debate about world affairs can only be understood in these terms. The actual situation of the country and the Bush administration is simple to the point of near transparency. The United States was attacked in September 2001 by an enemy whom we — i.e., Democrats, Republicans, and ordinary citizens — had not taken seriously enough. We were compelled to go to war — not metaphorical war, as Greeley vilely postulates, but real war — for multiple unassailable reasons. The tradition of personal liberty in this country means that there will never be a surefire way to detect and thwart terrorist threats within our borders. The only alternative to creating a police state is to go where the terrorists originate and kill, imprison, or frighten enough of them to reduce the threat to manageable proportions. The enemy is an amorphous worldwide entity, incarnated as individuals, schools, charitable organizations, mosques, paramilitary units, political parties, and nations. Because of our long inattention, our intelligence about the enemy is alarmingly poor. Were it otherwise, we would not have been devastated so unexpectedly on 9/11. In a single moment, all foreign policy assumptions were turned on their heads. Before 9/11, it seemed reasonable

71

to assume the best case until events proved otherwise. After 9/11 it became absolutely necessary to assume the worst until events proved otherwise. Make no mistake: it is not just the American economy but the world economy which cannot afford a mass destruction event in the United States, however shortsighted individual nations may be in their policy making.

Iraq was an avowed enemy of the United States, a proven aggressor, a proven developer and user of chemical/biological weapons. Our frighteningly scarce intelligence about Iraq could not prove to anyone's satisfaction that Saddam was not an imminent threat, was not in possession of an immediately usable stockpile of weapons of mass destruction, was not directly in cahoots with the other major Arab entity which insisted on calling us 'The Great Satan.' Much of the rest of the world was far less concerned about this, because their tears about 9/11 were crocodile tears from the start.

It is vital to understand that the key to the current situation is the very lack of intelligence that is now being used to assault both Tony Blair of the U.K. and George Bush. This is not the same as saying there was no intelligence. It is that the intelligence which did exist was piecemeal, contradictory, not at all reassuring, and more out of date than any potential combatant in a war wants the enemy to know about. Did George Bush and Tony Blair lie? By the standards of global politics, they were as carefully, nitpickingly candid as they could afford to be without rendering themselves impotent to eliminate the threat. This is a situation that requires the judgment of grownups, not whining children.

Time out for a quick review. The enemy is fundamentalist Islam, whose relation to so-called mainstream Islam and Arab ethnocentrism features boundaries so tenuous and subtle as to be invisible. Thus, all decisions about how to proceed against the enemy are fraught with risk and destined, regardless of which alternatives are chosen, to result in at least some negative consequences. Yet the greatest risk in the face of an unknown threat is inaction, the willingness to wait until a determined enemy makes its own choice about the next arena of conflict.

Therefore, the "unilateral" American invasion of Iraq. Astoundingly, a swift and brilliant military campaign with essentially no U.S. casualties and a remarkably fortunate (meticulous?) dearth of civilian casualties and infrastructure damage. The result? Occupation of a nation whose experience of war was so brief as to have left almost no scar, precious little appreciation of the hammerstroke that had been so deliberately left undelivered. That undelivered hammerstroke in part consisted of the absence of military mopping up, which in most full scale wars results in vividly ugly incidents. The desire to be humane resulted in the decision to leave too much of Saddam's military and political apparatus in the field. This was, of course, a deliberate gamble, and it was a gamble whose consequences were aggravated by an unanticipated (lack of intelligence again) decrepitude in the infrastructure of Saddam's Iraq. All the care taken in not destroying waterworks and electrical plants was wasted; these vital components of nationhood had already been destroyed by neglect.

Now it is four months later, and what is the situation we face as a nation?

By all rational standards the occupation is proceeding extremely well. To view the results of an in-depth poll of Iraqi citizens which I have nowhere seen reported in the mass media: CLICK HERE

Yet polls in our own nation suggest that the people are growing increasingly concerned about whether or not their president has done a good job. Why are they concerned? Because of an unending series of "Big Lies" being propounded by left/liberal citizens of the United States of America.

BIG LIE 1: America's unilateral action in Iraq turned the will of the world against us. (Click here for an outstanding analysis of this falsehood)

BIG LIE 2: George Bush lied us into a war with Iraq for no reason, unless it was about oil or lucrative business contracts for Republican political donors. Right. From the moment they take office, American Presidents are living in the history books. It's absurd beyond responding to to suggest that a man who is already rich and well connected would plunge himself into the cesspool of history by betraying the national interest in favor of a few business contracts.

BIG LIE 3: There were never any weapons of mass destruction, and Bush and Blair almost certainly knew and covered it up. Recall if you are able, the incontestable fact that even our whiniest foes in the U.N. never claimed there weren't WMDs in Iraq; their opposition consisted of not wanting to do anything about them. Even the Clinton administration's eight years of pronouncements about WMDs were squarely in accord with what the Bush administration and the U.N. believed.

BIG LIE 4: The occupation of Iraq has been irretrievably botched and has become a Vietnam-like quagmire. This is an absolutely ridiculous assertion. 60,000 Americans died in Vietnam over a 10-year period. Throughout that time, American troops faced a fully armed and centrally organized military opposition in the field. No comparison is even possible. Remember, too, that it took years to establish the conditions for self rule in both Germany and Japan after World War II. The only way our current situation can be viewed negatively is to insist, childishly, on no ill consequences for any of the gambles we take in combating terrorism, in which case we will do nothing until the dirty bomb at the Sears Tower kills 10,000 in Chicago.

BIG LIE 5: It's proof of American imperialist ambitions that the Bush administration has gotten along so poorly with the U.N. and still persists in hindering the U.N.'s right to oversee the rebuilding of Iraq. Again, an utter absurdity. The only consistent features of U.N. policy are its tacit support for Palestinian terrorists and its determination to poke a stick in America's eye at every opportunity. There is no seat of wisdom or benevolence that anyone can point to in this corrupt organization. Libya and Cuba occupy seats on the U.N.'s human rights commission. Who could ever trust this organization to administer any situation competently, fairly, or honestly? Every single reference by an anti-Bush politician to "the U.N." is a proof that there is no one at the U.N. worthy of the deference so fraudulently accorded that organization.

BIG LIE 6: The war on terror is now more dangerous than ever because terrorists are flocking to Iraq; the war, on balance, has made the situation worse. This "Big Lie" can be true only if the terror threat against America consists purely of al Qaida remnants in Afghanistan. To postulate this means assuming that Syria is not a terror threat, Iran is not a terror threat, and that Saddam's Iraq was never a harbor, training ground, organization site, weapons supplier, or financier for terrorists. All of these are demonstrably ridiculous and dangerous assumptions. It bears repeating that prudent foreign policy now consists of assuming the worst until it can be entirely disproved.

BIG LIE 7: The best evidence for believing all the darkest implications of numbers 1 through 6 lies in the extreme right wing policies pursued by the Bush administration in every area (because we all know what that means). Now, all of the lies are absurd, but this one is downright comical. By every standard but national security, George Bush is the most liberal Republican president in living memory. Indeed, he has supported and passed so many watered down versions of Democratic legislative programs that without the overriding national security concerns, he would in all likelihood be facing a conservative challenger for the 2004 nomination. Any Republican you speak to outside of New York, California, and New England is guaranteed to be hopping mad about multiple ways this President has steered to the left of his party's historical positions on limited government, education policy, entitlements policy, immigration policy, and perhaps most importantly, on the need for fighting back against liberal slanders and the liberals' low strategems in matters of legislation and judicial nominations.

What can be proved is that all of these purported lies are, in fact, lies. The proof consists of the utter absence of rational proposals from Democrat politicians or liberal media pundits about what might be done next, given the current set of circumstances, as opposed to what has already been done wrong in the reinvented past. The purposes the lies serve are: 1) to undermine the president's popular support at home, his credibility abroad, and his effectiveness in convincing our enemies — Iraqi resistance and Islamic terrorists both — that it is futile to hope for

Americans to quit. (All of these outcomes are directly contrary to the interests of the American people, our troops in the field, and our ability to act in concert with even our allies); and 2) to conceal the fact that the left/liberal character assassins in the Democratic party have no ideas of any kind about how to prosecute the war on terror — unless you count it an idea to transform the dismembered victims of the twin towers and the murdered marines in Tikrit into casualties of a purely "metaphorical" war.

If Hitler is anywhere on the scene in today's world, he resides in the persona of Saddam Hussein, who, in the eyes of all the rabid, lying Bush haters, can't hold a candle to George Bush for tyranny, duplicity, inhumanity, and selfish ambition. And what, may we ask, is this if it is not simply a monstrous joke? It is, we suggest, "the ruthless persecution and demonization of an imaginary enemy for purely political purposes." That's right; it's classic McCarthyism. The Democrat obsession with fascism is a triumph of narcissism, an unconscious self-indictment projected onto every adversary who obstructs their sense of entitlement to rule.

The lies I have enumerated here are stated or implied in every diatribe of the sort promulgated by Andrew Greeley and his despicable accomplices. The indignity and damage such lies wreak on the nation at this critical time in our history are so huge, so indefensible, and so far beneath contempt that it staggers the mind to try seeing them whole. Every one of the Democratic candidates for president has given at least lip service to multiple of these lies, and all of them should be treated to the scorn of the American public and a one-way ticket back to whatever hate-filled lair they call home. We should all demand that the remainder of the Democratic party field a list of replacement candidates capable of debating policy alternatives at home and abroad without impugning the motives of a president who has had to make innumerable difficult decisions in a time of unprecedented national crisis, with an unprecedented lack of support from the "loyal opposition." Any American who can sneer at the man who has had to bear this burden of transition into a brand new kind of world war is, to put it bluntly, stupid and undeserving of respect.

Mr. Greeley, if you have an ounce of personal integrity in you, you should remove that collar and mail it back to the pope. You're no Christian in any sense of the term. And I do mean that as an insult.

The Dinosaur Perspective

This latest entry requires a bit of setup because it began as a dialogue across the divide between conservatives and liberals. I discovered, on a "right-wing" website, a link to Pussification, a deliberately outrageous satirical essay by one Kim du Toit (kimdutoit.com), who delights in playing the unreconstructed male chauvinist gun nut. I found the piece funny, sharp and, in the way of good satire, incisively true in many essentials. Du Toit had also created a link to an extended dissenting opinion at a website called Philosoraptor (philosoraptor.blogspot.com). I read this essay as well and had a mixed reaction to it. The prose resonated with the usual liberal tone of superiority, and much of the argument marched down the predictable dogmatic path of secular egalitarian orthodoxy. Nevertheless, I sensed here and there an intent, an aspiration even, to be fair and even-handed: Philosoraptor went so far as to allow that du Toit's argument included elements that in less 'neanderthal' hands might be worthy of further thought. I also suspected that the attempt at even-handedness was being undermined by youth, naivete, or both. For example, he began his argument thus:

"I'm torn about Kim du Toit's essay about, as I'll put it, avoiding his gratuitous crudity, the wimpification of the Western male. I'm inclined to ignore it, since it's unlikely that anyone who found the essay insightful will listen to anything I have to say about it; but du Toit is full of shit, and that, combined with the apparent popularity of the essay on the right wing of the web makes it hard to ignore. I'm torn about it also because... I do think that the threat of wimpification is worth discussing. That's why it's too bad that du Toit's essay is such a piece of crap--the wimpification point gets lost in a torrent of bigotry, falsehoods, and right-wing fantasies."

I thought it laudable that he would consider up front the possibility that "wimpification is worth discussing." I thought it very X-gen that he would haughtily shrink from the word "pussification" and then use the word "shit" in the very next sentence. As he proceeded with his extended denunciation of anti-feminist reaction, I also found myself doing a double-take at a few of his assumptions:

"Conservatism is currently the Colossus of American politics. Extremist conservatives control the Presidency and both houses of Congress, and conservatives exercise virtually unchallenged control of the political agenda... Never in my lifetime has one end of the political spectrum so dominated American public life."

Let's see: the last time one party held the presidency and both houses of Congress was... 1992? And then there was this:

"Here's another textbook fallacy (note: sounds like "phallus," but means something different. And, although I know you think that using a phallus makes you smart, using a fallacy does the opposite.) This fallacy is called the "post hoc fallacy" from post hoc ergo propter hoc. That's Latin, which is an old language that smart people used to use. It means after this, therefore because of this. See, what you are saying is that government got bad after we foolishly started treating women as if they were human beings, letting them vote and suchlike. So, since it happened after women got the vote, it must have been women's voting that caused it. Textbook fallacy. Oops...I meant: textbook fallacy, dumbass. First, government has probably gotten less intrusive since women got the vote. The government has, since then, become less likely to interfere with sex acts between adults, abortion, and contraceptive use. It was, until recently, less likely to tell us what we could and couldn't read. But, far more importantly, the country has become far more just and fair since women got the vote—think about the Civil Rights and Voting Rights Acts of the early '60's. Since these were passed after women got the vote, should women get the credit for them? You know, men did have al little something to do with 'em. Especially Lyndon Johnson. You should like Johnson—he's a little like W. He's from Texas, and he lied to get us into a war. But he cared about civil rights, so he's different, too."

Government less intrusive since 1920? (Time out for head scratching.) I was convinced I was reading the work of a youngster, and so, looking past the actual subject of his diatribe, I sent Philosoraptor an email in which I suggested that his perceptions were distorted by ignorance attributable to his youth. I was somewhat patronizing but not hostile. I suggested that he suspend his automatic assumption of superiority over dinosaurs such as Du Toit and (by implication) me.

I promptly received a courteous reply from Philosoraptor. He told me I was mistaken in my assessment of his youth. He told me he was 40 years old. (More head scratching.) He shared some particulars of his background and upbringing. He reemphasized his scorn for du Toit but conceded he might have been wrong in his assertions about a trend toward less intrusive government. He also allowed that there were extremists at both ends of the political spectrum but opined that the extreme left had been effectively marginalized, while the extreme right had contrived to capture the center of political debate. He thanked me for writing.

Thereupon, I was moved to write the following:

Dear Philosoraptor,

I grant that 40 isn't a kid anymore, and I was initially surprised when you clocked in at that age, but it has caused me to rediscover an idea I've considered in the past. I am 50, older than you but only moderately so in chronological terms. Yet the idea I'll share with you is that the particular ten years of difference between us amount to a whole world of experience and perspective that is critically important.

I am not insulting the character of your youth and upbringing. I accept that they are as you say they are. Why, then, do you still strike me as naïve? For example, your email statement that the far right is now taking over the center, while the far left is marginalized sounds to me, well, ludicrous. Why?

The ten years I have over you takes in the American culture and politics of the late 1950s, the Cuban Missile Crisis, the assassination of JFK, the mounting protests against the Vietnam War, the sudden arrival of drugs, the semi-revolutionary generation gap between teenagers and parents, SDS, the Black Panthers, the RFK/MLK assassinations, feminism, Woodstock, Altamont, Kent State, Eugene McCarthy, George McGovern, and Watergate. Granted, you were also alive during some of this, but you were not witness to the extraordinary transformation of the country that happened in this short period of time, and you cannot know with real emotional conviction the "before" that gave way to the "after" we have all inherited.

Before the transformation, liberal Democrats were JFK and LBJ. They differed from conservatives in believing that government should be more activist in trying to ameliorate inequities in the population. They wanted bigger government, more federal controls of business, more federal law in areas such as civil rights. Republicans wanted less of all these things. Both Democrats and Republicans were united in their defense of the nation against foreign threats. Democrats wanted, perhaps, to spend less on defense, not because they wanted to undermine the military, but because they wanted more to spend on social programs.

It is popular now to regard the "before" era as a repressive, stultified dark age. For some percentage of the population, every age is a dark age. In every age, some constituencies suffer more injustices than others. This does not mean that every age is inherently without value and virtue. So it is with the "before" I remember that you cannot.

In the context of that time, your assertion that the far right has occupied the center is absurd. What happened in the 1960s was that the entire nation lurched, or was hijacked, left. What used to be a leftism so secret that it often accompanied membership in the Communist Party became the accepted left wing of the Democratic Party, which re-engineered the party's nominating process so that Democrats strong on national defense could never again be nominated. The influence of this part of the Democratic Party combined their reflexive responses to Vietnam and Watergate into a permanent hostility to the use of American military power overseas and to the executive branch, especially in matters of foreign policy and especially when Republicans held office.

In the "before" era, the current posture of the Democratic presidential candidates toward the president and his foreign policy would have been unthinkable. Harry Truman faced at least as difficult a situation in Korea as George Bush does now, with far fewer immediate national security issues at stake, and while he faced political opposition to his war policy, he was not accused of lying, cronyism, imperialism, self-aggrandizement, and fraud. JFK brought us so close to nuclear war that I can still remember days of direct, continuous cold fear, but in the aftermath, no one sought to turn his government inside out for the purpose of ridiculing his decision making and his honesty. I know you are itching to leap in here with your current events expertise to make the usual liberal case for why all these charges are true, but bear with me for a moment. Regardless of what merit you believe your case holds, what you cannot see is that the whole context in which it is socially acceptable to hate George Bush with the open venom you (or your colleagues, if I'm being presumptuous about you) display is a function of "after" -- after Vietnam, after Watergate. These events gave the permission for the politics of personal destruction, a kind of total war that could bring down even the President of the United States. That's right. It didn't start with Nixon. Or with Clinton. It started with demonstrators outside the White House in 1966: "Hey, hey, LBJ. How many kids did you kill today?"

You can argue all you want that it's better now, that the transformation was justified. I will contend that it wasn't, while allowing for opposing views. What I insist on is that much that was good has been lost. My father loathed JFK; during that president's term in office my father spent almost half his time overseas on business. And when he was on foreign soil, he refused ever to say a word against Kennedy or the policy of the U.S. government. Neither did his fellow Americans.

Many rank-and-file Republicans were bitterly disappointed that Nixon refused to contest what appeared to be flagrant voting irregularities in Mayor Daley's Chicago, which represented the county that gave JFK Illinois and the election. Nixon refused to turn the presidential election into a partisan legal battle because of the dangerous precedent it would set. Before. Politics at both the citizen and candidate level had some standards of decorum.

Other things have been lost as well, notably quality of life for the overwhelming majority of Americans. In the 1970s, this country embarked on the most radical social experiment ever attempted by a human society, without even allowing itself to recognize that it was an experiment. I'm referring to feminism. Five thousand years of accumulated traditions and roles were almost immediately junked. If you never knew the "before" it's easy to see why all this seems like it must represent all that is best in humanity — justice, freedom, equality, and so on. Yet it also seems that no one is counting the cost. The divorce rate has skyrocketed, illegitimate births have risen to astonishing levels, juvenile encounters with drugs, crime, and sex have moved from virtually nonexistent to epidemic, educational achievement has plummeted to near ruin, and a new statistic called "abortions per year" was developed, computed into the millions, and then banished from the pages of the almanac because we don't like counting it anymore. Do women at least seem happier to those of us who remember the "before"? No. They don't seem happier. Their marriages crumble, the new equality deprives them of the protections they used to enjoy in the event of divorce, their children are too often unsupervised, too often kidnapped by their unsupervised peers into addiction, sexual promiscuity, and premature cynicism. Further, women feel obligated to pursue careers that turn out to be — surprise! — tedious, stressful, wearying, and debasing (whether in the factory or the boardroom, the "Company's" most universal motive is debasement). They abandon age-old protections of dress, behavior, and speech, and — surprise! — they pay for it with date rape, violent assaults, the need for abortions, and worse.

And for some of us "before" dinosaurs, these kinds of unintended consequences aren't even the worst ones. What we failed to take into account in our unacknowledged experiment was the real socio-political role the nuclear family played in the culture — in every culture above the hunter-gatherer level known to recorded history. The few years a child has in the home with its mother and father before reaching serious school age, 6 or 7, is the only time when the goodness latent in that child can be developed without countervailing influences from institutional culture. It's a brief window during which parents can instill curiosity, manners, awareness of right and wrong, the meaning of responsibility, altruism, and honesty.

We have failed to understand that every organization in which we become members, all our lives, will exert amoral pressures that benefit the organization and work, directly or indirectly, to mold the identity of a person into a shape different from its initial individuality and humanity. That we have good and virtuous people who are ever proof against corruption, seduction, and greed is a function of what happens in those first six or seven years of life.

Now, we have enticed mother out of the house, away from her children (and please don't preach to me about economic necessity: there is absolutely no need for the exorbitant number of parentless households we now tolerate), and we have attempted to plug the ugly holes in the fundament of our culture with — what else? — new, more intrusive institutions of government, which reach deeply into that once private preserve of the home to monitor the children's welfare and begin the process of absorbing them into institutional identities at an earlier age than any society has ever attempted.

Perhaps the change in the children is not sinister or even detectable if you weren't there before. A close friend of mine has spent the last six years living in a household with a contemporary American teenager of good reputation and recognized academic and personal merit. He told me in a recent letter, "I have no doubt she has been trained so well in accordance with the accepted standards that if she chanced to become a junior executive, fresh out of B-school, with the Final Solution Corporation, she'd have no trouble managing the day-to-day schedules and operations reports of the divisional crematory. As long as she didn't have to work too much overtime and could phone in sick pretty often after an all-nighter with her current boyfriend."

Some of us, including "bigoted idiots" like du Toit, can't help remembering ladies. They were our mothers and grandmothers, our friends' mothers and grandmothers, and they had no idea they were prisoners of a vicious sexist culture. They knew how to smile, how to make strangers and shy ones feel welcome, they knew how to dress up for a party, how to dance to ballroom music, how to practice countless skills that made houses into cheery homes, and we loved them. In every possible way they exemplified the essential human virtues and mediated their children's vulnerability through their own. They were playing a life-and-death role, especially in those first six years, and one that fathers couldn't play because their role back then was different. Fathers weren't second-string mommies, always playing catch-up on the sensitivities not born into men. They were, when all was said and done, judges — the ones charged with preparing the children to be strong against the institutional temptations and corruptions that were coming after the time of safe haven was over. Their job was not to be taken in the way mother could be by an artful grin or pleading. Their job was to say no, to describe the consequences, to levy the punishment so that the lesson would be learned in the home, not in the dangerous realms of the outside world.

"Before" there were fathers and mothers. "After" we have "deadbeat dads" and a plethora of lawyers, doctors, journalists, executives, and bureaucrats, all with ticking biological clocks and an enduring confusion about the difference between home and government. If they can't be in the home, then they want the world as a whole made as safe as a home. They want more laws, more protections, more services. They beg the government to come deeper into the home, inside the car, into the chemistry of their children's brains. Your post hoc ergo propter hoc analysis is dead wrong. The women's vote has played a pivotal role in the rise of nanny government precisely because they're always looking back in the direction of a home that is no longer what it was.

And as I've said, you're perfectly welcome to prefer the "after" to the "before." It is just that the certitude you display about your preference for what has been a very recent drastic change is as shallow as it is rigid. The so-called return of the right-wing has not rolled back the clock in any material way in any part of the culture. GW Bush is proposing and signing levels of entitlement spending that would have made him a leftwing Democrat "before," and in his domestic policies generally he can only be called conservative by a contemporary leftist. Your apparent blindness to these contradictions in terms is what makes you seem naïve. And to some of us, probably, you also seem presumptuous in your automatic assumptions about the world reactionaries would like to have back, at least in part.

Doctors made housecalls. People who went out to dinner at nice restaurants dressed up for the occasion. Fathers were as stern about the importance of being a "gentleman" as they were about the importance of being a man. To hit a girl or to swear in public was not just wrong. It shamed you.

Shame was apparently a function of class oppression, because now there is no shame. Why did so many of us rightwingers hate

Clinton so much? Because he was obviously no gentleman, and the president should always be a gentleman (or a lady). Then he proved it and shamed the nation before the whole world. What did we rightwingers really want to happen with the Lewinski scandal? What we couldn't ever have. We wanted him to resign because that would have been the right and gracious thing to do. A fanciful archaic throwback of a notion? Maybe. But if Clinton had resigned, then perhaps President Gore might have focused more national attention on a certain piece of violent Arab street trash and prevented a few thousand deaths.

Funny how being a gentleman can sometimes also be a pragmatic and positive act. If Al Gore had been a gentleman like Nixon (!) before him, he would have disdained to contest the results in Florida. He would still have won his popular vote victory, despite the electoral defeat, and he would have been well positioned, even admired, as a candidate for 2004. (Pause: Compare this scenario with the erratic hide-and-seek irrelevancy Gore has since become.) Meanwhile Bush might have been spared the rancor and bile of the Democrats, and the new "tone" everybody had hoped for might have been achieved. And by the time foreign policy decisions became so horrendously critical, the Democrats might have had a respected advisory role to play.

Hell, they might even have played a respectable role. Instead of seething on the sidelines, characterizing every single presidential decision as a new low in corrupt right wing power politics. If a few more of our leaders had behaved like gentlemen, in fact, our foreign policy might be more successful at this very moment.

"Hey, hey, LBJ. How many kids did you kill today?" That's our tone. It's been our tone ever since. It was the tone of the 1968 Democratic convention in Chicago. It's the tone of civil rights leaders since the assassination of Martin Luther King (though it wasn't his tone). It was the tone of the Watergate scandal. It was the tone of about 2,000 book-length feminist screeds about men and the unfairness of being born with a uterus. It was the tone of the Reagan haters. It's the tone of both sides of the abortion debate. It was the tone of the Thomas and Bork hearings. It was the tone of the impeachment debate. It was the tone of the 2000 presidential election aftermath. It's the tone now. And some of us are tired of that tone precisely because we remember the time before it was there.

It's the tone of spoiled kids, boys and girls, who are just plain pissed at not getting their way, at not having every obstacle removed from their path by someone else. They should get their way because they're entitled. And we have made that principle the basis of our great secular religion, the religion of "after." Never mind the consequences. Even though the economics is slam-dunk against women in divorce, never mind that. Fire them up about their freedom to throw the bum out if he has an affair. Never mind that she, and her kids, will be paying for his affair forever. And by the way, don't teach the boys about being a gentleman — even in courtship and marriage — because that's an elitist term, and if we start talking about gentlemen, then somebody else might be tempted to start talking about ladies, and everyone knows that women have to be free to do whatever in hell they want, regardless, damn the consequences, because that's what equality is all about. And if they want, they can dress like sluts from grade school on, and talk like sluts from grade school on, and act like sluts from grade school on, and do all the drugs that any slut might want to do, and have as many abortions as any slut would want to have,.and marry the first idiot who asks, and divorce him when he cheats, and marry the next one, and maybe do some cheating herself, and have a kid, and divorce the next one, and then set up shop as a bitter single mother who has it on good authority that all men are no-good bums. Now, how about all those government programs she'll need to get by as a single working mother...? And isn't this absolute paradise compared to the days when women weren't free, and men weren't permitted — by their fathers or each other — to be total, irresponsible slobs?

In fact it's all working so well that we can try another experiment, and start bringing the boys up to be more like girls, so that they can dress like sluts from grade school on, and talk like sluts from grade school on, and act like sluts from grade school on, and do all the drugs that any slut might want to do, etc etc. After all, the only difference is that girls have sockets and boys have plugs, and they can start connecting to one another (and calling each other slut and ho and bitch) from grade school on, because that's what freedom and self esteem are all about. And look at all the other progress we get with this approach: no more toy guns, double the cologne sales, and a fantastic new growth market in condoms.

Of course it's better. That's how we can be absolutely sure it's okay to sneer at the idiot Republicans who hearken back to the evil racist sexist "before," because we all know what they really miss is being able to use the N-Word on the servants, and commit secret incest with their daughters, and treat their wives like slaves, blah, blah, blah.

And because we also know that it's very very dangerous to allow ourselves to consider, for even a moment, that maybe most women were better suited to the old way, and maybe only a small percentage actually belong out here in the nasty rough-and-tumble, and maybe our kids and all our home lives would be better, happier, if we could admit that the nuclear family is the indispensable foundation stone of an entire civilization, and that dynamiting it away without a single forethought might have been a criminally stupid thing to do.

But no. It's always been this way. For everyone 40 and younger. It's the right way. The conservatives are stupid, bigoted, immoral, and wrong. "Hey, hey, LBJ. How many kids did you kill today? Not as many as we're going to kill in the next 50 years..."

Forgive me. Yes, we get heated. That's because we're so stupid. And wrong. And immoral. Maybe you could bear that in mind, and treat us dinosaurs with a little kindness. Like a gentleman.

About the Author

R. F. (Robert) Laird was born in Salem, New Jersey, the son of a World War II fighter pilot and the grandson of a World War I infantry captain. As a member of the notorious Baby Boom generation, he came of age during the late 1960s and witnessed firsthand the radicalization of American college campuses, the explosion of the drug culture, and the sexual revolution. He was educated at Harvard University and went on to do graduate work at the Cornell University business school, where he observed former radicals and hippies rededicating their lives to the pursuit of material prosperity.

After pursuing a successful career as a management and communication consultant, Laird took a sabbatical from the world of business in the late 1980s to complete a work of satirical fiction he had begun nearly 10 years previously. *The Boomer Bible, A Testament for Our Times,* was published in October 1991 by Workman Publishing of New York and was named by the *Wall Street Journal* as one of the 10 most significant books published that year.

Laird has since published *Shuteye Town 1999* and *Shuteye Nation,* both blistering multimedia topical satires published at the multiple blogs, including InstaPunk and the website Deerhound Diary. He also has 20 books available at Amazon.

Meanwhile, R. F. Laird continues to work and write from his home in Salem, New Jersey.

Made in the USA
Middletown, DE
18 November 2020